UX for Recommendation Systems in E-Government
A Checklist to Enhance User Experience

by
Will Gimenes

For whom is this book intended

Computer and User Experience (UX) Specialists
It facilitates the optimization of recommendation systems on government portals.

Interface Designers
The book can assist these professionals in designing more intuitive and efficient interfaces, ensuring that government digital services are user-friendly and accessible to everyone.

Digital Project Managers
It enables managers to make more informed decisions and prioritize the most critical aspects of the project.

Students and Researchers
The work covers up-to-date literature and presents a practical checklist that can be applied in various contexts.

Digital Marketing Specialists
It provides ways to increase user engagement and trust, crucial elements for the success of any digital initiative.

Public Policy Analysts
It contributes to the creation of more efficient public services focused on citizens' needs, positively impacting the population's quality of life.

Prologue

This book addresses the creation of recommendation systems (RS) for digital government portals, with a focus on user experience (UX). Although part of the content specifically deals with the solution implemented in Brazil, the gov.br portal, it is important to note that this portal is internationally recognized as a reference in digital government. The Brazilian experience in developing gov.br serves as a valuable case study, as it demonstrates the practical application of concepts and techniques that can be adapted and used in different contexts.

Most of the content in this book is dedicated to universal themes for UX professionals, such as interface usability, system transparency, accessibility, data protection, accuracy and diversity of recommendations, user engagement, situational and linguistic dimensions, project maturity, and cognitive effort. By exploring these themes, the book offers a UX checklist for recommendation systems in digital government portals. This checklist is designed to assist specialists in creating more efficient, user-friendly, and relevant systems for citizens, regardless of country or culture.

INTRODUCTION

In recent years, many government services that were previously conducted in physical locations or over phone calls have transitioned to digital platforms. In this context, the gov.br portal was established in Brazil in 2019 as a central hub for accessing federal government news and services. Initially offering around three thousand services, the need arose to implement a recommendation system to facilitate the search for specific services, thereby reducing the effort required by users.

The primary function of this system is to predict, in some way, the most urgent needs of users. Recent studies indicate that providing a good experience with recommendation systems depends not only on the accuracy and variety of suggestions but also on other factors beyond the algorithms. These factors include interface usability, the clarity of the information presented, transparency about how the system works, user data protection, and a focus on accessibility.

Integrating all these elements, which span different areas, is a significant challenge in creating a more satisfying user experience. To ensure the success of the recommendation system on the gov.br portal, computer and user experience (UX) specialists continuously work to find technical solutions that enhance the system. In this context, using a checklist that considers various aspects of user experience can lead to a more pleasant and efficient interaction.

In this book, we present a UX checklist for recommendation systems in digital government portals. This checklist brings together various items from different areas that are essential for the effectiveness of these systems.

E-GOVERNMENT, RECOMMENDATION SYSTEMS, AND USER EXPERIENCE

In addition to the general outlines of each area, we address their interrelationships, taking into account the perspectives of contemporary authors.

E-GOVERNMENT

The emergence of a more democratic and inclusive expansion of government services has led to the creation of e-government initiatives[1]. These can be understood as efforts by government information technology agencies to transform their relationships with citizens, businesses, and other areas of the government itself. The technologies employed aim to provide higher quality services as interactions between parties become more effective and efficient. This type of governmental action can also potentially reduce corruption, increase transparency, foster economic growth, and decrease public spending (World Bank, 2022).

---

[1] The term 'e-government' is often used synonymously with 'digital government,' but this is not a unanimous view in the academic environment. Some authors believe that e-government refers to the use of ICTs to improve the services delivered by governments. In contrast, digital government represents an evolution of e-government as it further optimizes processes. In this book, we will use the two terms interchangeably, as a detailed discussion on their distinctions falls outside the scope of this work.

International organizations have published reports on the maturity level of e-government across all continents. Biennial studies by the UN assess the development of e-government in its 193 member countries. Among these studies, the E-Government Development Index (EGDI) stands out, comprising data from the organization itself and other UN-associated agencies. The index is formed by three dimensions: one related to the country's telecommunications infrastructure, another referring to human capital, and a third linked to the level of online services available in each country (UN, 2022). The data on human capital are obtained from UNESCO studies. In the report referring to the year 2022, it becomes evident that the countries best positioned are also those with greater political stability, economic development, and more democratic regimes (Gillies, 2005; Feng, 1997). Denmark ranks first with a score of 0.9717, considering that the scale ranges from zero to one. Countries with similar political and economic situations present comparable index values, such as Finland, Australia, and the Netherlands. Brazil ranks 49th with a score of 0.7910, an index that strongly suggests a deficiency regarding infrastructure, as this component had the lowest value among the three, as can be observed below: 0.8964 for online services, 0.7953 on the human capital index, and 0.6814 for telecommunications infrastructure (UN, 2022).

Another index that measures the level of development of e-government in countries is the GovTech Maturity Index (GTMI), which consists of 48 indicators, one of which is the previously mentioned EGDI. The index focuses on foundational government systems, improvements in service delivery, citizen engagement, and instruments for promoting e-government (World Bank, 2022). In this index, 198 countries are grouped by letters according to their score in the GTMI. Brazil is in the highest-ranked group, which corresponds to 35% of the evaluated nations, totaling 69 economies in this category. The average GTMI score is 0.552 on a scale ranging from zero to one. Brazil achieved a score of 0.975, ranking just behind South Korea, which scored 0.991. There are countries among the top 10 positioned, such as Saudi Arabia, whose government, however, does not have a democratic regime (CLITEUR and ELLIAN, 2020).

There is also a relevant index called the Digital Government Index (DGI), provided by the Organisation for Economic Co-operation and Development (OECD), which assesses the maturity level of digital government strategies among member and partner countries. The index consists of four transversal facets: strategic approach, policy levers, implementation, and monitoring (OECD, 2020). In this index, South Korea leads with a score of 0.742 on a scale ranging from zero to one. Brazil ranks 16th, considering that the OECD has 32 members and that Brazil is one of the four evaluated countries that are not part of the organization but has key partner status (OECD, [n.d.]).

It is possible to see how much each method used influences the position of countries within each index. It is important to note that Brazil's performance has varied considerably, but the country's indices have been improving (UN, 2018, 2022). The presented indices help to situate Brazil's level of development in terms of e-government and allow for observation that Brazil occupies a position close to other major economies in the world regarding e-government practices. However, there are also shortcomings, primarily of a structural nature (UN, 2022).

RECOMMENDER SYSTEMS

Recommender systems were created in the 1970s (SANTINI, 2020), with some independent initiatives utilizing similar principles (RICH, 1979; TERRY, 1993). These systems emerged with the intention of helping people make better and easier choices in catalogs of any kind (XIAO and BENBASAT, 2007; RESNICK and VARIAN, 1997 apud CHAMPIRI, 2019; KNIJNENBURG, 2012), and consequently, increasing user satisfaction (KNIJNENBURG, 2012).

Some important principles of recommender systems stem from the observation of a very common human behavior: trusting the recommendations of people close to us about which movie to watch or which book to choose. Often, people also consider letters of recommendation in recruitment processes or read reviews from critics in newspapers to determine whether a play is worth seeing (KNIJNENBURG, 2012).

The term "Recommender System" was solidified in its definition in the late 1990s by Paul Resnick and Hal R. Varian (RESNICK and VARIAN, 1997 apud CHAMPIRI, 2019), and music media were the first to be tested with the algorithms of that time. The vibrant collaborative environment that existed at a time when social networks were not yet widely disseminated in society contributed to the development of this field of knowledge (SANTINI, 2020).

In companies that offer a large number of items for users to select from, recommender systems play a fundamental role. According to Netflix, 80% of the movies watched on the platform are chosen based on recommendations from the system; meanwhile, about 40% of clicks on Google News come from recommendations (SANTINI, 2020). On the sales website Amazon.com, 35% of the items purchased were selected due to some recommendation made by the company (MACKENZIE et al., 2013).

Among the various aspects involved in the development of a recommender system, one relates to customization. Depending on the scenario, if it is possible to capture user data, recommendations can be made based on browsing history. If obtaining such data is not feasible, recommendations are based on general user preferences (SUN et al., 2021) or on approximate requirements.

Recommender systems use various techniques to identify which items may be of interest to users. Among these techniques, the following stand out: content-based filtering and collaborative filtering, which is further divided into model-based filtering and memory-based filtering. The latter is subdivided into "user-based" and "item-based" filtering. Additionally, there are hybrid approaches (ZAHRAWI, 2021).

Content-based filtering

Recommender systems, which use filtering techniques to present relevant information or products to specific users, can operate based on content. They learn to suggest items similar to those that users have previously shown interest in. By analyzing the defined characteristics of each item, the system identifies those with the highest similarity and presents them as options to the user (RICCI et al., 2011). An example of this type of filtering is when a user purchases a book by a particular author, and the system begins to recommend other works by the same author.

Collaborative filtering

Recommender systems based on collaborative filtering can collect data either implicitly or explicitly. In the case of implicit collection, information is obtained by analyzing various moments in the user's journey, such as clicks, scrolls, and views. On the other hand, explicit collection requires an intentional action from the user that demonstrates their experience in a specific situation, such as rating an item (SUN et al., 2021). An example of this type of filtering occurs when a user expresses a negative opinion about a particular item in a forum. Based on this collaboration, the system begins to exclude similar items from its recommendations.

Model-based filtering

The model-based approach utilizes information that is present but not immediately obvious or visible. An example would be recommending a podcast whose hosts are both sarcastic and scientific, without the user explicitly expressing preferences related to those classification terms (RICCI et al., 2011).

Memory-based filtering

This method is based on the trust that the user has in people close to them. By considering the choices of these so-called "neighbors," it is possible to predict the interests of the user in question (YU et al., 2004). For example, if a group of users shares similar tastes, such as an appreciation for a particular type of wine, and users A, B, and C have all purchased wine X, while only users A and B have also acquired wine Y, there is a reasonable probability that user C will also like wine Y. For this reason, the system will recommend this item to them.

Hybrid filtering

Each technique has its advantages and disadvantages, and hybrid systems utilize combined approaches in an attempt to compensate for the deficiencies of each and enhance their positive characteristics (BURKE, 2007).

Artificial intelligence in recommender systems

Recommender systems with artificial intelligence have benefited from various techniques to address the growing demand for recommendations in light of the vast amount of information that falls under the domain of what is known as big data. The approaches used help to tackle issues such as data sparsity in certain circumstances, adaptation to dynamic environments, and integration of different sources of information (ZHANG et al., 2021).

GOV.BR AND ITS RECOMMENDER SYSTEM

In this chapter, we provide a brief history of e-government in Brazil and how the recommendation system of gov.br was developed, from the perspective of the experts involved.

Brief history of e-government in Brazil

The e-government program of the Brazilian federal administration was created in 2000, when a working group composed of representatives from different ministries was established with the goal of examining and presenting solutions related to the electronic ways in which the state and citizens connect. During the analyses conducted by the group, a situation was identified in which various initiatives lacked integration.

In 2008, the Brazil e-GOV Standards were introduced as guidelines for best practices organized in manuals, aimed at improving communication and the provision of electronic information and services by federal government agencies. The first manual to be published was the coding manual.

Continuing the progress toward the adoption of a comprehensive platform, in 2013, the federal government introduced the Digital Government Identity, a design initiative aimed at establishing a standardization in the appearance of government websites to enhance communication with citizens (MINISTÉRIO DA GESTÃO E DA INOVAÇÃO EM SERVIÇOS PÚBLICOS, 2019).

In August 2019, the federal government launched the gov.br portal, which aimed to gather approximately 3,000 electronic government services in the shortest time possible (SERPRO, 2019). The service was created by the then Ministério da Gestão e da Inovação em Serviços Públicos[2] in association with Serpro - Empresa Nacional de Inteligência em Governo Digital e Tecnologia da Informação[3].

The solution, implemented as a portal, was established based on the guidelines outlined in a 2016 decree, which encompasses various directives on the provision of digital public services. This platform enables users to initiate and process requests, provided they are available in digital format (DE ALENCAR et al., 2022).

n 2023, gov.br reached the milestone of 150 million registered users and offers approximately 4,000 services (AGÊNCIA BRASIL, 2023).

At the beginning of 2025, the portal already offers 4,510 services and has 169 million accounts (GOVERNO DIGITAL, 2025).

Recommender system on gov.br

---

[2] in English: Ministry of Management and Innovation in Public Services.
[3] In English: National Company for Digital Government Intelligence and Information Technology

In the case of the recommender system, the implementation history in Brazil points to more recent contexts. Specific information about the implementation of these systems was obtained through inquiries with federal government experts who participated in the deployment of gov.br. In its first version, released in 2021, the goal was to handle access by unauthenticated users. If the same user accessed the platform through different means, they would be treated as a distinct user because their access was not being recorded for the recommender system.

In the second version, the capability to capture the needs of authenticated users was incorporated, allowing the system to unify its view of them.

In the third version, artificial intelligence procedures were incorporated, enabling a more precise understanding of users' needs and, consequently, providing more accurate recommendations. The statistical data used to generate recommendations are obtained through Google Analytics and an internal database that records whether the user has actually used a particular service. Each database contains information weighted by a specific data set, which helps determine the ranking of the suggested recommendations.

Considering Figure 1 – Table of gov.br Recommendation Types and the findings from expert inquiries, it is evident that the services displayed in the "Most Accessed" and "Highlights" columns necessarily do not appear in the "Recommended" section. This is due to a guideline that prevents redundancy in this element. The reason why each column is there is related to a specific need.

Figure 1 – Table of gov.br Recommendation Types

RECOMMENDED	MOST ACCESSED	HIGHLIGHTS
Extração de dados da Plataforma Lattes	Consultar CPF	Cultura, Artes, História e Esportes
		Bolsa Atleta
	Assinatura Eletrônica	
Validar e assinar documentos		Educação e Pesquisa
	Consultar CNPJ	Inscrição no ProUni (ProUni)
Diretório de Grupos de Pesquisa		
	Consultar Meu Imposto de Renda	Trabalho, Emprego e Previdência
Emitir certidão de regularidade fiscal		Concurso Público Nacional Unificado (CPNU)
	Obter a Carteira de Trabalho	
Cadastrar e realizar assinatura eletrônica de documentos	Consultar dados do Cadastro Único	Defesa Civil e Defesa Nacional
		Serviço Militar Obrigatório (SMO)
Submissão na Plataforma Brasil de projetos de pesquisa envolvendo seres humanos para avaliação ética		Educação e Pesquisa
		Inscrever-se no SISU (Sistema de Seleção Unificada) (SISU)

Source: reproduction taken from the gov.br website in 2025.

Regarding the methods used for the gov.br recommender system, both collaborative filtering and content-based filtering are applied.

In terms of UX practices used in the creation and implementation process, the approach included user journey mapping, discovery meetings, accessibility testing, prototype testing, design system, personas, and the analysis of statistical access data to identify trends and behaviors.

Regarding the UX metrics involved in the project, the following were used: Conversion Rate, Customer Satisfaction Score (CSAT), Drop-Off Rate, and Time on Task.

User Experience

The relationship between users and products or services can be referred to as user experience (UX). The term refers to a subjective outcome shaped by a user's specific perspective, previous experiences, and the context of each interaction (KNIGHT, 2019).

The design of objects and services takes into account the interaction between people and technology. This experience can lead to either satisfaction or frustration, depending on how the objects and services are conceived. When designing for people, it is essential to understand both psychology and technology (NORMAN, 2013).

A well-designed project requires effective communication between objects or services and users. It is essential that these designed elements indicate what actions can be taken, what is happening, and what will happen next (NORMAN, 2013). The UX Honeycomb, created by Peter Morville, presents a series of key aspects that contribute to user-centered design. It suggests that products or services should be:

- Useful: Items should solve a user's problem, considering that their needs and behaviors change over time.
- Usable: Objects or services should be easy to learn and use, with interfaces playing a fundamental role in this aspect.
- Desirable: This aspect is strongly linked to emotional elements and the user's connection with the identity of products and brands.
- Findable: Everything the user wants to search for should be easily located.
- Accessible: Accessibility should be ensured for all users, regardless of whether they have any disabilities.
- Credible: Products must be designed in a way that makes them trustworthy.
- Valuable: The product should provide value both to users and to the business (MORVILLE, 2004 apud KNIGHT, 2019).

Image 2 - Peter Morville's User Experience Honeycomb

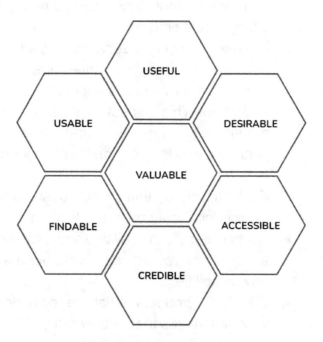

Source: Adapted from Morville's original.

A factor that influences user experience is related to interfaces, more specifically usability. This term refers to the evaluation a user makes when using a machine or software, considering how simple or complex the operation is. Usability can be divided into five components:

- Learnability: How difficult it is for the user to complete basic tasks from the first use.

- Efficiency: How quickly users perform tasks after learning how to use the system.
- Memorability: After a period of not using the system, how difficult it is for the user to resume using it.
- Errors: How many errors the user makes while performing tasks.
- Satisfaction: How enjoyable the interface is to use (NIELSEN, 2012).

There is also the perspective that, to achieve better usability, it is essential to minimize the efforts associated with reading, screen scrolling, finding items, clicking and tapping, typing, waiting for page loading, shifting focus of attention, and the amount of information that needs to be remembered to complete a task (Budiu, 2013).

It is necessary to separate the usability component from the user experience. An example to establish this difference would be a certain interface allowing movies to be found with few steps, however, providing few reviews of movies from a certain genre. The act of searching is easy, but the result is frustrating. In this case, the interface is evaluated positively, but the experience is bad (Nielsen, 2012).

UX *Writing* - making reading easier

Digital interfaces have their own unique characteristics that require dedication from professionals specialized in the field. The texts within these interfaces are found in menus, definitions, buttons, chatbots, and error messages, among others. The small portions of text in each of the examples are called microcopy (COURSERA, 2023). It is argued that these elements should be concise and direct to provide the user with the best possible experience (RODRIGUES, 2019). The words or sentences must be strictly tied to the actions that lead the user to make a particular decision. They should also provide instructions for the desired action, and there is a need for the user to receive textual feedback after performing an action (YIFRAH, 2017).

The relevance of microcopy in the user experience is linked to the fact that, before the digital era, the only entities that communicated verbally were humans. Whenever verbal communication was established, our minds associated this event with a human, and this relationship created an emotional connection with the other party, motivating us to act. When establishing verbal communication with an interface that mimics human communication, this emotional connection presents itself in the same way. To ensure smooth interaction, it is essential that the interface elements adhere to social conventions and that the words used are conversational, that is, they represent the type of language used in human dialogue (YIFRAH, 2017).

Regarding clickable texts, it is important to understand that they can contribute to making content easily findable and should be accessible to all users. For the result of the click to be satisfactory, it is essential to produce microcopy that is as precise as possible while remaining concise. Links, on the other hand, represent a promise to access a specific address, which interfaces must fulfill (MORAN, 2019).

On the web, it is unlikely that users will read your content in its entirety or in a linear manner. Therefore, it is useful to accept that texts will be scanned. For each part to be found efficiently, the content should be placed in a visible, clear, and prominent location. It is also necessary to use text blocking techniques, such as lists, along with simple language (MORAN, 2020).

Métricas de UX

It is possible to evaluate the user experience by considering various aspects, including behavioral ones. A practical example would be measuring the time a user takes to create an event on their smartphone calendar. Another crucial aspect for evaluation is attitudinal factors, such as when someone expresses their opinions through comments about a specific application. Additionally, there are aspects that require special equipment to be measured, such as eye-tracking to detect which areas of the screen are of greater interest (ALBERT and TULLIS, 2022).

In the context of user experience research, or UX Research, formative and summative analyses are possible approaches to evaluate usability and user satisfaction. Formative analysis is conducted during the development of a project and provides inputs to adjust the product throughout the development process. Summative analysis, on the other hand, occurs after the product is completed and aims to evaluate the overall effectiveness of a product or service. It is particularly useful for identifying improvement opportunities in the pre-launch phase of a solution (ALBERT and TULLIS, 2022).

Personal preferences play a significant role in evaluating the user experience. Measuring these preferences is crucial for designing enhanced experiences. One user might prefer a particular element to be larger, while another might prefer it to be smaller, and neither of these interface solutions is necessarily right or wrong; they simply align more or less with the individual tastes of each user (ALBERT and TULLIS, 2022).

Producing solutions that are easy to use is no longer sufficient to generate pleasant experiences for users. It is necessary to create positive emotional responses in users to increase their engagement and trust in the brand or product. Some emotions are closely associated with interactions with products. It is believed that seven emotions play a predominant role in the user experience:

- Engagement: Refers to the level of emotional involvement of the user with the product.

- Trust: Relates to the trust a user places in a company, reflected through its products or services. Transparency plays a fundamental role in this relationship.
- Stress: Measures the level of stress or pressure that interacting with a particular application may generate while performing a task.
- Joy: Relates to the satisfaction and happiness a user feels upon completing a task. This experience is directly linked to the perceived difficulty of the task; generally, lower cognitive load results in greater joy.
- Frustration: Reflects the sense of helplessness experienced when a user is unable to complete a task.
- Trust: Can be built based on the degree of certainty provided by accurate feedback after completing a task.
- Surprise: Indicates how unexpected events can positively or negatively contribute to the user experience (ALBERT and TULLIS, 2022).

Recommendation Systems and UX

Several factors impact the user experience in their interaction with recommendation systems. The accuracy of recommendations is fundamental for satisfaction, anticipating user preferences. Diversity enriches the suggestions, avoiding limitations to items that are very similar to those previously transacted. The inclusion of new items in the recommendations over time is essential to make them attractive, and the introduction of unexpected elements is desired by users seeking variability. Transparency is crucial for establishing trust between users and the platform, and the context of the recommendation enriches the results (RICCI et al., 2011). According to researchers, the interface can have a more significant impact on user satisfaction than the performance of the algorithms. Personal and situational characteristics, as well as concerns about data privacy, also play relevant roles in user satisfaction (KNIJNENBURG et al., 2012).

Regarding accuracy, many believe that more efficient algorithms result in superior recommendations, which would lead to higher user satisfaction. However, recent studies indicate the presence of other subjective elements that also influence the user experience (KNIJNENBURG, 2012).

When it comes to the diversity and degree of novelty offered in the results of recommendation systems, it is understood that in the case of a user who has already shown interest in a particular title, it is assertive not to recommend only items from the same family, as this may make the recommendation too limited and useless. Moreover, the results need to display some degree of novelty in relation to the items, as this practice attracts more user interest and increases their satisfaction. However, it is prudent to keep the level of recommendations for new items low, as this may result in suggestions that are too random, which would generate a poor experience. Serendipity plays a crucial role in the user experience, expanding the recommendation options. Its absence creates a problem known as the "filter bubble," which forcibly restricts the suggested universe, making it less attractive. Therefore, it is advisable to include unexpected yet relevant items for the user, contributing positively to the experience (PARDOS, 2020).

Transparency is a characteristic that can increase user satisfaction because when users are informed about how the system works and are invited to intervene in the recommendations by making adjustments and providing feedback (JANNACH et al., 2017), this practice increases trust (RICCI et al., 2011; GONZÁLEZ CAMACHO, 2020).

Context also influences the quality of the recommendation, as it can enrich suggestions that are sensitive to certain circumstances, such as a clothing store offering more suitable clothing for the season and during vacation periods (RICCI et al., 2011).

Studies indicate that a visually simple and easy-to-understand interface contributes to greater user appreciation of the platform (PU et al., 2011; RICCI et al., 2011). The experience can also be positively impacted when the interface efficiently utilizes computational resources, especially when they are more limited (RICCI et al., 2011). When considering the platform as a whole, and not just the design of the recommendation system interface, one should be aware that design problems can influence the evaluations of the suggested items on the platform, resulting in a negative effect on the recommendation results (SONG et al., 2012).

Adjustable preferences regarding interaction methods in recommendation systems depend on personal characteristics such as domain knowledge, which refers to the level of understanding a user has about a particular subject or specific area. The propensity to trust the solution presented by a recommendation system is affected by domain knowledge. Well-informed users may be more critical of suggestions, while those with less knowledge may accept recommendations more readily. This means that the more a system understands users' domain knowledge, the more effective it will be in making relevant and personalized suggestions.

To enhance the user experience in interactive recommendation systems, it is essential to understand each user's control needs. However, it is important to consider that providing too many adjustments or highly complex ones can increase the user's cognitive effort, leading to reduced satisfaction with the system (JIN et al., 2018).

Although users have their general preferences and this data is opportunely used in a recommendation system, situational characteristics also have the power to influence the experience. Depending on the context, such as the location where the person is, their home, the city where their job is located, or the weather conditions, it is possible to obtain additional information that contributes to improving the quality of the recommendations (RICHTHAMMER et al., 2020).

Recommendation systems utilize user data to generate personalized recommendations. However, the indiscriminate use of this information can negatively impact privacy, causing users to feel that the system retains more information than needed (RICCI et al., 2011). Users must trust that the data necessary for making recommendations are well-protected. By instilling this confidence, platforms convey a sense of loyalty, which helps to retain their user base (PU et al., 2012).

It is essential to develop solutions that use user data sparingly while ensuring that this information is not accessible to other users (RICCI et al., 2011). It is worth remembering that the restrictions established in Brazil by the General Data Protection Law - LGPD (similar to the European GDPR - General Data Protection Regulation) regarding data privacy require a review of what data and to what extent recommendation systems can use in the recommendation process (GONZALEZ CAMACHO, 2020).

Accessibility, Recommendation Systems and UX

Accessibility, defined by Brazilian Law 10,098 as the ability to safely and autonomously reach spaces, furniture, urban equipment, buildings, transportation, and communication systems by people with disabilities or reduced mobility, encompasses two distinct aspects that are subject to similar challenges: physical and digital (TAVARES FILHO et al., 2002).

In the context of web accessibility, ensuring easy access for anyone, regardless of physical conditions, technical means, or devices used, is fundamental. The development of an accessible website involves following web standards, adhering to accessibility guidelines or recommendations, and conducting accessibility evaluations. These measures are essential to promote digital inclusion and ensure that everyone has equal access to online information (EMAG, 2014)[4].

To ensure the accessibility of web content for people with disabilities, it is crucial to follow some recommendations. First, it is important to provide informative and unique titles for each page, highlighting relevant information. The use of headers is recommended to convey meaning and structure, providing a clear outline of the content. Alternative and meaningful text should be included for images, describing information or functions. Writing should be simple and clear, with short sentences and paragraphs, avoiding complex language. Link text should be descriptive of the destination, and clear instructions should be provided (W3C.ORG, 2023).

---

[4] The EMAG (Accessibility Model in Electronic Government) is an initiative of the Brazilian Federal Government aimed at promoting digital accessibility on government websites and portals. It consists of a set of recommendations to ensure that digital services and content are accessible to the largest possible number of people, regardless of their physical, sensory, or cognitive abilities.

The color of elements, despite being a relevant component, should not be the only visual means of conveying information, indicating an action, requesting a response, or distinguishing a visual element (W3C.ORG, 2018). Considering color and contrast, the color difference between the background and the foreground content, whether text or another component, should be sufficiently large to ensure legibility. When designing legible interfaces for different visual abilities, it is assertive to follow the WCAG guidelines and use a contrast checking tool, such as webAIM (MOZILLA.ORG, [n.d.]).

In terms of UX, there is a strong correlation between solutions with a high degree of accessibility and the feeling of being close to and included in the system. Thus, projects that are properly developed and tested for accessibility will provide more satisfying experiences for users (AIZPURUA et al., 2016).

Checklist Practices

Checklists are valuable tools for quickly verifying specific items. These products boost productivity by providing a comprehensive overview of the tasks to be performed. By listing and organizing activities, it becomes possible to prioritize the efficient use of time and avoid forgetting essential tasks (COSTA et al., 2021). Furthermore, checklists promote a stimulus for productivity, generating a positive feeling for having completed the activity, encouraging continuity, and increasing overall efficiency. The regular adoption of checklists results in a noticeable reduction in the mental load required to remember daily microtasks, contributing to more effective time and responsibility management (CANVA.COM, [n.d.]). When developing a checklist, it is also assertive to consider that it should be designed with a user-centered approach to ensure it does not become an unpleasant activity for those who will use it (NORMAN, 2013).

There are some practices that enhance the quality of a checklist:

- Define your objective: It is assertive to indicate whether the verification will be optional or mandatory, which audience will use it, and the purpose of the check.
- Invite users for initial tests: It is necessary to have access to the people who will use the checklist to ensure the relevance of the checks.
- Be clear: The checklist should use expressions that are easy to understand and do not leave room for many interpretations.
- Keep it concise: It is crucial to keep the checklist as efficient as possible, checking the maximum number of useful items while maintaining simplicity and economy of characters to avoid making the task tedious.

- Continuous testing: For the checklist to maintain its effectiveness, its content must be tested and eventually updated, following the needs of users and technological developments (KASEYA.COM, [n.d.]).

CHECKLIST FOR RECOMMENDATION SYSTEMS IN DIGITAL GOVERNMENT

In this chapter, we discuss the definitions of the proposed checklist, explaining the reasons behind the suggested items and analyzing its components individually, elucidating the potential benefits for the user when implemented in a project.

Checklist Definitions

The implementation and use of checklists are highly relevant for areas of knowledge that require operational standards, such as medicine and aviation. Checklists offer a reduction in the complexity of executing certain tasks, provide low-cost reference resources, and considerably help in reducing failures in procedures with many steps and varying difficulty (GAWANDE, 2023). Our proposal offers a checklist for specialists involved in creating recommendation systems for digital governments. It takes into account multidimensional factors related to the user experience that can contribute to increasing satisfaction more effectively, compared to a one-dimensional view, that is, one that only considers the **accuracy** of algorithms, for example, although this cannot be excluded from a checklist proposal of this nature (RICCI et al., 2011; PU et al 2012). Three factors were adopted due to their relevance justified by some authors. The first is the dimension of **engagement** (ALBERT and TULLIS, 2022; JANNACH et al., 2017;

RODRIGUES, 2019), as it expands the user's contact with the service. The other is the dimension of **trust**, which contains elements such as the transparency of the service's operation or the security regarding the processing of personal data that the service performs (RICCI et al., 2011; GONZALEZ CAMACHO, 2020). The next dimension is **accessibility**, because as AIZPURUA et al. (2016) point out, it increases user satisfaction by facilitating access to information for users with disabilities. We also present four other dimensions, formulated from guidelines pointed out by NORMAN, (2013), KNIJNENBURG et al. (2012), RICCI et al. (2011), CORTÉS-CEDIEL et al. (2017), CHAMPIRI (2019), and JIN et al. (2018), as well as from my personal experience as a graphic designer and UX practitioner. These dimensions are project **maturity**, **situational** dimension, **cognitive effort** dimension, and **linguistic** dimension. In summary, we propose that the checklist be composed of 8 dimensions:

- Algorithm accuracy
- Engagement
- Trust
- Accessibility
- Project maturity
- Situational dimension
- Cognitive effort
- Linguistic dimension

Regarding the number of items, the proposal covers **14 aspects** that aim to address various aspects of the user experience related to a digital government recommendation system. They take into account attributes worked on by contemporary authors cited in this study and within the scope of the book.

Our checklist can be used with two approaches. The first is formative application, which takes place in the project development phase when the team is collecting data to provide input to the UX research team. At this point, the checklist can offer insights and creation guidelines to guide design decisions, aiming to more effectively meet user needs. The second form of application is summative, which can happen in the pre-launch phase of the project, when it is necessary to perform checks of various natures before putting the project into production. This allows for possible modifications to be made and, at the same time, to carry out a comprehensive evaluation of the product, aiming at future improvements (ALBERT and TULLIS, 2022). For each item on the proposed checklist, the evaluator should only mark those which they believe have been implemented to some degree, even if only partially. Each item also has an auxiliary text that contributes to its understanding, justifying its necessity and providing examples when needed.

How to use the checklist

A simple way to implement the use of the checklist is to create a simple HTML file with all the items described.

The person responsible for the check marks all those that are included in their project and, at the end, clicks on a check button. The result is a linear score from zero to one hundred percent. Due to a matter of scope of the study, we have not yet defined percentage ranges to characterize the level of compliance in relation to the verified items. Each user of the checklist must adopt a standard, according to the project's requirements.

Checklist Components

Next, we present the checklist items and comment on their functions. Each item consists of a question that takes into account some important aspect of UX, followed by a brief explanation of what type of benefit it can offer to the user. The order of the items follows a grouping similar to that presented in previous chapters, organized by affinity whenever possible. After presenting each item that can be part of an HTML file, we provide further explanations regarding why it is important to consider that particular aspect. These explanations are not intended to be part of the checklist itself but rather serve as additional context and justification for the inclusion of each item.

Item 1: Has the project undergone a benchmarking process compared to other digital government solutions that meet similar needs? (Conducting constant

benchmarking reduces the ideation workload
and puts the user in a privileged position).

Notable international organizations, such as the UN, OECD, and World Bank, conduct studies on the level of maturity of countries in their digital government implementations. These analyses address various criteria to assess the progress of each nation in digital services. Although Brazil has made progress in some aspects, there are still deficiencies in several evaluated items (VIANA, 2021). It is assumed that the countries that rank higher in these studies have more advanced recommendation systems (OECD, 2020). Therefore, it is important to examine these possible implementations in order to establish a reference for updating Brazil's digital government recommendation systems. It can be said that this item considers the dimension of project maturity, because as best practices are incorporated, the service is expected to be more efficient, consequently leading to user satisfaction.

Item 2: Does the project incorporate more than one type of filtering in the algorithm? - (Recommendation systems that use combined algorithms tend to have better accuracy. E.g., content-based filtering, demographic filtering etc.).

Recommendation systems can use a variety of approaches with respect to the algorithms employed. Each code has its own characteristics with advantages and disadvantages. One approach that can promote improvement in the accuracy of recommendations and consequently increase user satisfaction is to combine more than one algorithm that contributes to the same process, making the solution hybrid (RICCI et al., 2021). It is understood, therefore, that the specialist will have a more successful project if they choose an approach that combines more than one filtering method, considering the available data for this purpose. This item primarily deals with the dimension of algorithm accuracy, as its effectiveness is directly linked to user satisfaction.

Item 3: Does the application allow the user to explicitly declare their personal interests and make configuration adjustments? (Enabling the user to convey this information increases engagement).

Providing a satisfactory user experience is linked to several components, including the opportunity for each user to express their content and solution configuration preferences. Additionally, it is beneficial to allow the user to inform their personal characteristics, which may not always be detectable through navigation tracking. Enabling the user to transmit this information explicitly can be a driver of the engagement dimension in relation to the solution (JANNACH et al., 2017).

Item 4: Does the solution inform about how the recommendation is made? (E.g., 'this item was recommended because you said you have item X'. This approach promotes increased trust).

Transparency plays a crucial role in the trust that the user places in a recommendation system. Detailing the recommendation process with a certain degree of specificity can increase the likelihood of the user choosing the suggested item while generating positive emotions (GE et al., 2022 and GONZALEZ CAMACHO, 2020). In this item, it is considered that the dimension of trust can be positively affected, as informing how the recommendation system works can generate satisfaction.

Item 5: Does the project take into account the user's residence or current location? (Detecting where the user is located can provide valuable information, such as the possibility of promoting targeted vaccination campaigns).

Digital government services may experience variations in demand based on regional contingencies. For instance, promoting vaccination campaigns may be more critical for affected populations based on the characteristics of their dwellings. Furthermore, it is possible that a user is temporarily in a city far from their residence due to work reasons, and in that location, a campaign to assist with banking access is taking place, which could be useful for them (Cortés-Cediel et al., 2017). In this scenario, taking into account the situational dimension means detecting where the user is and being able to provide valuable information in temporary circumstances.

Item 6: Does the system take into account seasonal variables? (Several parameters can increase the quality of the suggestions presented, such as using data on harvest seasons, rainy seasons, or vacation periods).

In the context of seasonality, several parameters can influence the suggestions presented by the recommendation system. It becomes imperative to use more predictable events as instruments for promoting specific services, especially those most needed at certain times and locations. For example, the grain harvest schedule follows a predetermined calendar throughout the year. On the other hand, during spring and summer (from April to September in the Northern Hemisphere), there is a higher incidence of Lyme disease cases, which requires specific alerts and dissemination of care. During holidays and festive periods, there is a decrease in vehicle traffic, while several city halls promote outdoor activities for families that can be better publicized. During these periods, there are also professions with greater demand; therefore, it would be opportune to anticipate this need for labor through the promotion of training for workers (CORTÉS-CEDIEL et al., 2017). These listed possibilities relate to the situational dimension, considering that the events occur in specific and predictable episodes.

Item 7: Does the project consider the probable needs of the user's stage of life? (It is possible to promote services that relate to needs based on age, such as vocational training, vaccination schedules, and retirement).

There are specific needs that vary according to each individual's age. These demands can be met by promoting services related to momentary issues, the need for vocational training, the personal and children's vaccination schedule, and information about retirement (CORTÉS-CEDIEL et al., 2017). Considering the data that can be cross-referenced from various public agencies, but always respecting the limits of local data protection legislation, it would be possible to scale personalized recommendations with this set of variables (KNIJNENBURG et al., 2012). These items relate to the situational dimension.

Item 8: Does the solution consider the user's circumstantial needs? (Some examples would be: temporarily receiving a pension, being unemployed, being out of the country, etc).

An additional way in which recommendation systems can provide benefits to users is by considering the temporary context in which they find themselves (CORTÉS-CEDIEL et al., 2017). There are several opportunities to improve the experience by leveraging circumstantial information, such as being temporarily out of the country for a few months. When accessing the recommendation system, suggestions can be adjusted to prioritize likely needs, such as performing passport-related activities (RICCI et al., 2021). We understand that these needs are linked to the situational dimension due to their episodic nature.

Item 9: Does the system allow the suggestions presented by the recommendation system to be evaluated or criticized by the user? (Allowing suggestions to be questioned increases user trust).

Offering the opportunity to criticize the solution contributes to obtaining insights aimed at improving algorithms, interface, and other characteristics of recommendation systems. Furthermore, this practice increases user satisfaction, as they perceive that the environment is receptive to their personal considerations (JANNACH et al., 2017; PU et al., 2012). This characteristic also plays a crucial role in strengthening the dimension of trust and promoting a sense of belonging, as it creates a fluid relationship between the system and users.

Item 10: Does the system ask the user if the number of recommended items is adequate? (There may be too many or too few items, and allowing this criticism enables the system to adjust to the user's cognitive capacity).

When generating recommended item suggestions, it is necessary to consider the density of information presented on the screen. A very small list of recommended items may result in a low probability of meeting the user's needs. On the other hand, presenting an excess of items can lead to cognitive overload, resulting in dissatisfaction (CHAMPIRI, 2019). In this sense, it is noticeable that questioning the user about the desired number of items and adjusting it according to their preferences can significantly increase their satisfaction (JANNACH et al., 2017; PU et al., 2012). We believe the proposed item is related to the engagement dimension, as it promotes a closer relationship between the user and the system when it allows itself to be modified. We also understand that it refers to the cognitive effort dimension, given that this item allows adjustments to be aligned with the perceptual limits of each user.

Item 11: Is the solution capable of altering its language based on the user's level of education, regionalisms, or domain knowledge? (Adapting to the user's language increases their satisfaction. For example, SNAP, food stamps, nutrition assistance, or government food aid all mean the same thing to people with different experiences).

The adaptation of language, especially in the interface microcopies and recommendations, can enhance the effectiveness of information transmission, thus promoting user engagement and satisfaction (RODRIGUES, 2019; YIFRAH, 2017). This approach requires specific attention as it considers individual lexical regionalisms, literacy levels, and knowledge domains. Let's take the term 'food stamps' as an example. A person could perform a search on a government website using this term, and from that moment on, associating this search with what is known about that user, the recommendation system should employ the same term to offer suggestions for services or information related to the topic. However, another citizen with the same need could use the expression 'Food Vouchers'. Similarly, a doctor could search for 'SNAP - Supplemental Nutrition Assistance Program', and the recommendation system should act in an analogous manner when presenting suggestions. There are still other expressions that have the same meaning, and it is crucial that the algorithm takes into account the searches performed, along with the user's personal information, to prioritize the presentation of results in the language most familiar to the user of the solution. We believe that this item deals with the language dimension, as adjusting to the user's way of expressing makes the experience more satisfactory, despite requiring an increased development effort to be implemented. It also relates to the cognitive effort dimension, taking into account that people with lower literacy levels have interpretive limitations that affect the understanding of suggestions from a recommendation system.

Item 12: Does the system make it explicit that the personal data used are stored securely and used for a specific purpose? (Users who are insecure about the use of their data tend to refuse permissions. Therefore, it is crucial to communicate transparently about the security of storage and the specific purpose of the data).

The application must make it explicit that personal data processed for recommendation purposes are stored securely and have a specific purpose. If the data requires authorization to be used, it should be requested whenever necessary, and the user may have the freedom to revoke it at any time, depending on the local data protection law. Users who do not feel secure about the use of their data are less likely to grant permission for its use (KNIJNENBURG et al., 2012; RICCI et al., 2011). In these cases, the data used will not have the same scope, resulting in lower quality recommendations. It is considered that the trust dimension is favorably affected by this item as the system transparently informs about how the data is handled. In addition, it also conveys credibility by stating why the data is secure.

Item 13: Do the recommendations offered by the system include items that may be new to users? (The application should present unexpected items that are still relevant to the user. This approach helps users break out of their personal "bubble" and increases their satisfaction).

There are studies indicating that it is necessary to present items that do not belong to a domain too closely related to the user in order to enrich the results and broaden the user's interest in the suggestions. The software should present unexpected items that are still relevant to the user (RICCI et al., 2011). This approach helps users break out of their personal "bubble" and introduces something new, which can expand their knowledge repertoire. The proportion of results in this category should be moderate;

otherwise, it may create a sense of randomness. When used in the right measure, it enhances engagement, as users expect some degree of novelty, which helps keep them more connected to the solution.

Item 14: Regarding accessibility, has the solution been evaluated using any accessibility testing tool compliant with WCAG guidelines? (It is imperative to consider aspects related to information organization, interface, and language used. To meet this requirement, automated verification tools can be used).

When designing a digital solution, accessibility emerges as a crucial field of knowledge, requiring an approach aligned with the needs of people with disabilities. It is imperative to consider aspects related to information organization, interface, and language used. To verify whether the system adequately meets WCAG guidelines, the solution can be evaluated using automated testing tools (MOZILLA.ORG, [n.d.]). Although these tests do not replace evaluations conducted by real users, they play an essential role in reducing accessibility gaps, contributing to this dimension. This aspect of accessibility can also enhance user satisfaction, particularly for those with disabilities.

The following image illustrates a possible layout for the HTML page.

Checklist for E-Government Recommendation Systems

Check all items that were addressed in the recommendation system project, even if partially.

☐ 1 - Has the project undergone a benchmarking process compared to other digital government solutions that meet similar needs? (Conducting constant benchmarking reduces the ideation workload and puts the user in a privileged position)

☐ 2 - Does the project incorporate more than one type of filtering in the algorithm? (Recommendation systems that use combined algorithms tend to have better accuracy. E.g., content-based filtering, demographic filtering etc.)

☐ 3 - Does the application allow the user to explicitly declare their personal interests and make configuration adjustments? (Enabling the user to convey this information increases engagement)

☐ 4 - Does the solution inform about how the recommendation is made? (E.g., 'this item was recommended because you said you have item X'. This approach promotes increased trust)

☐ 5 - Does the project take into account the user's residence or current location? (Detecting where the user is located can provide valuable information, such as the possibility of promoting targeted vaccination campaigns)

☐ 6 - Does the system take into account seasonal variables? (DSeveral parameters can increase the quality of the suggestions presented, such as using data on harvest seasons, rainy seasons, or vacation periods)

☐ 7 - Does the project consider the probable needs of the user's stage of life? (It is possible to promote services that relate to needs based on age, such as vocational training, vaccination schedules, and retirement)

☐ 8 - Does the solution consider the user's circumstantial needs? (Some examples would be: temporarily receiving a pension, being unemployed, being out of the country, etc)

☐ 9 - Does the system allow the suggestions presented by the recommendation system to be evaluated or criticized by the user? (Allowing suggestions to be questioned increases user trust)

☐ 10 - Does the system ask the user if the number of recommended items is adequate? (There may be too many or too few items, and allowing this criticism enables the system to adjust to the user's cognitive capacity)

☐ 11 - Is the solution capable of altering its language based on the user's level of education, regionalisms, or domain knowledge? (Adapting to the user's language increases their satisfaction. For example, SNAP, food stamps, nutrition assistance, or government food aid all mean the same thing to people with different experiences)

☐ 12 - Does the system make it explicit that the personal data used are stored securely and used for a specific purpose? (Users who are insecure about the use of their data tend to refuse permissions. Therefore, it is crucial to communicate transparently about the security of storage and the specific purpose of the data)

☐ 13 - Do the recommendations offered by the system include items that may be new to users? (The application should present unexpected items that are still relevant to the user. This approach helps users break out of their personal "bubble" and increases their satisfaction)

☐ 14 - Regarding accessibility, has the solution been evaluated using any accessibility testing tool compliant with WCAG guidelines? (It is imperative to consider aspects related to information organization, interface, and language used. To meet this requirement, automated verification tools can be used)

Send

FINAL THOUGHTS

We consider that a recommendation system development project for digital government should take into account various aspects related to the analysis of government portals with the highest scores in evaluations by international organizations. These highly rated websites can indicate directions and solutions that contribute positively to the evolution of already implemented projects, as well as the development of new initiatives of this kind. Another relevant aspect concerns the sets of algorithms related to recommendations. There are various available models, each with its own advantages and weaknesses. Combining them seems beneficial for achieving more effective results regarding user experience. Additionally, factors such as engagement, trust in the system, the user's situation, region, age group, cognitive effort, linguistic attributes, concerns about personal data protection laws, and accessibility can influence the user's level of satisfaction. Developers must consider as many of these aspects as possible to increase the likelihood of a satisfying user journey when interacting with a government portal that includes a recommendation system. We understand that the percentage score generated by the proposed checklist can be part of a set of user experience metrics used during the project's development.

This book is an extension of a specialization monograph in UX, and we hope it will be useful to a broad range of professionals working in the field of user experience.

WORKS CITED

AIZPURUA, Amaia; HARPER, Simon; VIGO, Markel. **Exploring the relationship between web accessibility and user experience**. International Journal of Human-Computer Studies, v. 91, p. 13-23, 2016.

AGÊNCIA BRASIL. **Gov.br: governo quer expandir uso de plataforma até o fim de 2023**. 2023. Retrieved October 27, 2023, from https://agenciabrasil.ebc.com.br/radioagencia-nacional/gera l/audio/2023-07/govbr-governo-quer-expandir-uso-de-plataf orma-ate-o-fim-de-2023.

ALBERT, Bill; TULLIS, Tom. **Measuring the User Experience: Collecting, Analyzing, and Presenting UX Metrics**. 3. ed. Morgan Kaufmann, 2022.

BUDIU, Raluca. **Interaction Cost**. 2013. Retrieved November 10, 2023, from:https://www.nngroup.com/articles/interaction-cost-defin ition/

BURKE, Robin. **Hybrid web recommender systems. The adaptive web: methods and strategies of web personalization**, p. 377-408, 2007.

CANVA.COM. **The ultimate guide to creating a checklist**. [s.d.]. Retrieved November 23, 2023, from: <canva.com https://www.canva.com/learn/ultimate-guide-creating-checkli st/>.

CHAMPIRI, Zohreh Dehghani et al. **User Experience and Recommender Systems**. In: 2nd International Conference on Computing, Mathematics and Engineering Technologies (iCoMET). Sukkur, Pakistan, 2019. p. 1-5.

CLITEUR, Paul and ELLIAN, Afshin. **The Five Models for State and Religion: Atheism, Theocracy, State Church, Multiculturalism, and Secularism**. ICL Journal, vol. 14, no. 1, pp. 103-132. 2020.

COSTA, Chrystyane Campos et al. **Construção e validação de checklist para sala operatória como dispositivo de segurança do paciente**. Cogitare Enfermagem, v. 26, 2021.

CORTÉS-CEDIEL, María E.; CANTADOR, Iván; GIL, Olga. **Recommender systems for e-governance in smart cities: state of the art and research opportunities**. In: Proceedings of the International Workshop on Recommender Systems for Citizens (CitRec '17). Association for Computing Machinery, New York, NY, USA, 2017. Article 7, 1–6.

COURSERA. **What Is a UX Writer? Writing for the User.** 2023. Retrieved November 20, 2023, from https://www.coursera.org/articles/whats-a-ux/.

DE ALENCAR, Rafael Odon; PITA, Marcelo; AGRA, Ronaldo. **Sistema de Recomendação do Portal gov. br.** In: Anais do X Workshop de Computação Aplicada em Governo Eletrônico. SBC, 2022. p. 85-96.

EMAG. **eMAG - Modelo de Acessibilidade em Governo Eletrônico.** 2014. Retrieved November 23, 2023, from https://emag.governoeletronico.gov.br/.

FENG, YI. **Democracy, Political Stability and Economic Growth.** British Journal of Political Science. 1997.

GAWANDE, Atul. **Checklist: como fazer as coisas bem-feitas.** Rio de Janeiro, Sextante, 2023.

GE, Yingqiang et al. **Explainable fairness in recommendation.** In: Proceedings of the 45th International ACM SIGIR Conference on Research and Development in Information Retrieval. 2022. p. 681-691.

GILLIES, David. **Democracy and economic development.** Institute for Research on Public Policy 2005.

GONZALEZ CAMACHO, Lesly Alejandra. **Sistema de recomendação baseado na relação de amizade entre**

usuários de redes sociais num cenário de cold-start.
Tese de mestrado. Universidade de São Paulo. 2020.

GOVERNO DIGITAL. **Números do Governo Digital**.
Retrieved February 13, 2025, from
https://www.gov.br/governodigital/pt-br.

JANNACH, D., Ludewig, M., Lerche, L.: **Session-based
item recommendation in e-commerce: On short-term
intents, reminders, trends, and discounts**. User Model.
User Adapt. Interact. 27(3–5), 351–392 (2017)

JIN, Yucheng; TINTAREV, Nava; VERBERT, Katrien.
**Effects of personal characteristics on music
recommender systems with different levels of
controllability**. In: Proceedings of the 12th ACM
Conference on Recommender Systems. 2018. p. 13-21.

KASEYA.COM. **Checklist best practices**. [s.d.]. Retrieved
November 23, 2023, from
https://helpdesk.kaseya.com/hc/en-gb/articles/44074688742
57-Checklist-best-practices/.

KNIGHT, Westley. **What Is User Experience?. UX for
Developers: How to Integrate User-Centered Design
Principles Into Your Day-to-Day Development Work**, p.
1-12, 2019.

KNIJNENBURG, Bart P. et al. **Explaining the user experience of recommender systems**. In: User modeling and user-adapted interaction, v. 22, p. 441-504, 2012.

MACKENZIE, Ian; MEYER, Chris; NOBLE, Steve. **How retailers can keep up with consumers**. McKinsey & Company, 2013.

MINISTÉRIO DA GESTÃO E DA INOVAÇÃO EM SERVIÇOS PÚBLICOS. **Linha do Tempo**. 2019. Retrieved October 27, 2023, from https://www.gov.br/governodigital/pt-br/estrategia-de-govern anca-digital/do-eletronico-ao-digital.

MORAN, Kate. **Better Link Labels: 4Ss for Encouraging Clicks**. 2019. Retrieved November 10, 2023, from <https://www.nngroup.com/articles/better-link-labels/>.

MORAN, Kate. **How People Read Online: New and Old Findings**.
2020. Retrieved November 10, 2023, from <https://www.nngroup.com/articles/how-people-read-online/>.

MOZILLA.ORG. **Color Contrast**. [s.d.]. Retrieved November 23, 2023, from https://developer.mozilla.org/en-US/docs/Web/Accessibility/Understanding_WCAG/Perceivable/Color_contrast/.

NIELSEN, Jakob. **Usability 101: Introduction to Usability**. 2012. Retrieved November 10, 2023, from https://www.nngroup.com/articles/usability-101-introduction-to-usability/.

NIELSEN, Jakob. **Writing Style for Print vs. Web**. 2008. Retrieved November 10, 2023, from https://www.nngroup.com/articles/writing-style-for-print-vs-web/.

NORMAN, Don. **The design of everyday things revised and expanded edition**. Basic Books, New York, US, 2013.

OECD, **Digital Government Index: 2019 results**, OECD Public Governance Policy Papers, No. 03, OECD Publishing, Paris, 2020.

OECD.ORG. **OCDE América Latina e Caribe - Programa Regional**. Retrieved November 8, 2023, from https://www.oecd.org/latin-america/OECD-LAC-Regional-Programme-Information-Note-PRT.pdf.

PARDOS, Zachary A.; JIANG, Weijie. **Designing for serendipity in a university course recommendation system**. In: Proceedings of the tenth international conference on learning analytics & knowledge. 2020. p. 350-359.

PU, Pearl; CHEN, Li; HU, Rong. **A user-centric evaluation framework for recommender systems**. In: Proceedings of the fifth ACM conference on Recommender systems, Barcelona, Spain, 2011, p. 157-164.

PU, Pearl, CHEN, Li, and HU, Rong. **Evaluating recommender systems from the user's perspective: survey of the state of the art**. Springer Science+Business Media, 22(4):317–355. 2012

RICCI, Francesco; ROKACH, Lior; SHAPIRA, Bracha; KANTOR, Paul B. **Recommender Systems Handbook**. 1ª ed. New York, Dordrecht, Heidelberg, London: Springer-Verlag, 2011.

RICH, Elaine. **User modeling via stereotypes**. Cognitive science, v. 3, n. 4, p. 329-354, 1979.

RICHTHAMMER, Christian; PERNUL, Günther. **Situation awareness for recommender systems**. Electronic Commerce Research, v. 20, n. 4, p. 783-806, 2020.

RODRIGUES, Bruno. **Em busca de boas práticas de UX Writing**. Rio de Janeiro: Edição do autor, 2019.

SANTINI, Rose Marie. **O Algoritmo do Gosto: Os Sistemas de Recomendação On-Line e seus Impactos no Mercado Cultural: Volume 1**. Curitiba: Appris, 2020.

SERPRO. **Governo lança o Portal Gov.br**. 2019. Retrieved October 20, 2023, from https://www.serpro.gov.br/menu/noticias/noticias-2019/governo-lanca-portal-gov.br.

SONG, Yading; DIXON, Simon; PEARCE, Marcus. **A survey of music recommendation systems and future perspectives**. In: 9th international symposium on computer music modeling and retrieval. 2012. p. 395-410.

SUN, Ninghua; CHEN, Tao; GUO, Wenshan; RAN, Longya. **Enhanced Collaborative Filtering for Personalized E-Government Recommendation**. Applied Sciences, v. 11, n. 24, p. 12119, 2021.

TAVARES FILHO, J. P. et al. **Aspectos ergonômicos da interação com caixas automáticos bancários de usuários com necessidades especiais características de idosos**. In: Congresso Iberolatinoamericano de Informática Educativa Especial. 2002.

TERRY, Douglas B. **A tour through tapestry**. In: Proceedings of the conference on Organizational computing systems. 1993. p. 21-30.

UN. **United Nations e-government Survey 2018: Gearing E-Government To Support Transformation Towards Sustainable And Resilient Societies**, Department Of

Economic And Social Affairs, United Nations, New York, 2018

UN. **United Nations e-government Survey 2020: Digital Government in the Decade of Action for Sustainable Development**, Department Of Economic And Social Affairs, United Nations, New York, 2020

UN. **United Nations e-government Survey 2022: The Future Of Digital Government**, Department Of Economic And Social Affairs, United Nations, New York, 2022

W3C. **Diretrizes de Acessibilidade para Conteúdo Web (WCAG) 2.1**. 2018. Retrieved November 23, 2023, from https://www.w3c.br/traducoes/wcag/wcag21-pt-BR/.

W3C. **Writing for Web Accessibility**. 2023. Retrieved November 23, 2023, from https://www.w3.org/WAI/tips/writing/

VIANA, Ana Cristina Aguilar. **Transformação digital na administração pública: do governo eletrônico ao governo digital**. Revista Eurolatinoamericana de Derecho Administrativo, v. 8, n. 1, p. 115-136, 2021.

World Bank. **WBG GovTech Maturity Index 2020: The State of Public Sector Digital Transformation**, Washington, DC. World Bank, 2020.

World Bank. 2022. **GovTech Maturity Index, 2022 Update: Trends in Public Sector Digital Transformation**. Equitable Growth, Finance and Institutions Insight - Governance;. © Washington, DC. http://hdl.handle.net/10986/38499 License: CC BY 3.0 IGO.

XIAO, Bo; BENBASAT, Izak. E-**commerce product recommendation agents: Use, characteristics, and impact**. MIS quarterly, p. 137-209, 2007.

YIFRAH, Kinneret. **Microcopy: The Complete Guide**. Haifa: Nemala, Israel, 2017.

YU, Kai; SCHWAIGHOFER, Anton; TRESP, Volker; XU, Xiaowei; KRIEGEL, Hans-Peter. **Probabilistic memory-based collaborative filtering**. IEEE Transactions on Knowledge and Data Engineering, v. 16, n. 1, p. 56-69, 2004.

ZAHRAWI, Mohammad; MOHAMMAD, Ahmad. **Implementing recommender systems using machine learning and knowledge discovery tools**. Knowledge-Based Engineering and Sciences, v. 2, n. 2, p. 44-53, 2021.

ZHANG, Qian; LU, Jie; JIN, Yaochu. **Artificial intelligence in recommender systems**. Complex & Intelligent Systems, v. 7, p. 439-457, 2021.